Tomáš Míček
Elisabeth Kellner

PALOMINOS
AUSTRIA'S HAFLINGER HORSES

Text by
Dr. Hans-Jörg Schrenk

SUNBURST BOOKS

Flowing blonde manes in the fog: the herd of young stallions from the Ebbs stallion breeding centre in the Tirol, about 1,100 metres up the Niederalm.

Preceding pages: Haflingers were originally mountain horses. Even today in their land of origin they are driven up to the Alpine pastures to a height of 1,000-3,000 metres in the summer. The mares and foals spend months there without any human contact.

Today, as a result of years of careful breeding, this small, compact mountain horse represents an ideal leisure horse, for riding or driving. The Haflinger is good-natured but lively. The characteristic features of this breed are its chestnut colouring and its white mane. The Haflinger's noble head clearly indicates the influence of one its ancestors, the Arab.

At Ebbs, the stallion breeding centre of the Tirol Breeders' Association, the young stallions spend most of the warmer summer months up in the Alpine pastures until they reach the age of two. There in the broad expanses of the flat pastures, they develop completely naturally, out of reach of man's influence and they become accustomed to the rugged environment, growing to be tough and hardy. Their games and playful fights establish the hierarchy within the herd.

*The ideal stallion of Haflinger breeders: elegant head - long,
flowing white mane - chestnut colouring with white points.*

Written records dating back to the Middle Ages contain references to small, tough mountain horses in the southern Alps. These horses were reported to be quite different from the cold-blood horses found on the north side of the Alps. They were used as wagon horses and packhorses to transport loads to the isolated villages and farms of the mountain communities. This breed probably evolved from repeated cross-breeding between the indigenous race of horses and the Arab thoroughbreds which had been introduced into the area which is now Austria as a result of the crusades and wars against the Turks. The official birth of the Haflinger breed, however, was declared in 1874. In this year the stallion, 249 Folie, was born, a son of the Shagya Arab stallion, 133 El'Bedavi XXII. 249 Folie is the original ancestor of all Haflinger stallions registered since that time. It didn't take long before the progeny of this stallion aroused the interest not only of horse breeders in general, but also of those authorities in the government who were concerned with horse-breeding, and consequently the systematic breeding of Haflingers was introduced with state support. This was based on state registration of stud stallions. In 1904 the first Haflinger breeders' association was established with the aim of improving the breed and setting up a list of stud stallions and mares. The attractive characteris-tics of the Haflinger aroused the interest of more and more breeders, and soon the horses were also being bred on a wide scale north of the Alps, particularly in the bleak mountain valleys of the north Tirol. The first, near fatal turning-point in Haflinger breeding came in 1918, when the south Tirol was separated from Austria, following the First World War. At that time most of the breeding mares were in the south Tirol, whilst almost all the stud stallions were in Austria. It was only with great difficulty that the breeders in the south Tirol and Austria succeeded in resolving this situation.

However, the breed received a boost in 1938, when the German army bought a large number of Haflingers as packhorses for their mountain troops. At this time breeding of Haflingers started in Bavaria, introduced and supported by the army administration. The army founded a number of stables where they reared Haflinger foals brought from Austria.

From 1945 onwards there was a gradual change in the aims of the Haflinger breeders, who became concerned with breeding a more flexible horse, suited to a variety of uses, such as riding, driving and agricultural work. Although there was a reduction in the stock of all horses throughout Europe between 1950 and 1970, the Haflingers continued to win new fans and there are now over 100,000 Haflingers worldwide.

The energy which has
built up during a few days
standing in the stable
bursts out in a series of
wild leaps and gallops.

Today the main Haflinger breeding area is in the north Tirol in Austria. The breeding of Haflinger thoroughbreds has taken place there since the beginning of this century. The goal of the breeders is to produce a versatile recreational horse. The ideal height of the horses is 138-148 cm, or 142-150 cm for stallions. The Haflinger should be a square, stocky horse with an expressive, refined head, a well proportioned neck and clearly defined withers. The croup should not slope too sharply and should not be too conspicuously divided. The legs should be well muscled with pronounced joints.

Two young stallions undertake a mutual skin care routine. Usually two horses who are particularly friendly with each other do this. They nibble carefully at the skin on the neck and back of the other horse in the places which he can't reach, thereby getting rid of troublesome insects or, in the spring, an itchy winter coat.

It is hard for the mares and foals to find
food on the bare mountainside about
2,500 metres above sea level. Even in
the middle of summer it often snows
heavily up here and the horses have to
seek food under the snow.

In the Alpine pastures food is sparse but nourishing and ideal for horses.
The grasses and herbs contain large amounts of minerals which aid the
growth of the foals.

The mares and foals peer curiously at the photogapher. They very rarely see people this high up the bleak, treeless mountainside.

The birth of Haflinger foals usually takes place out in the open of the Alpine pastures without human help or intervention. This newly born foal lies helplessly, while its mother licks it dry.

Just a few hours after they have been born, the foals are able to follow their mothers everywhere. This four week old foal already strays quite far from his mother and is curious to investigate everything which he encounters on his wanders.

While the Tirol Haflinger breeders succeeded in transforming the Haflinger from a stocky pack-horse, similar to coldbloods, into a refined, versatile recreational horse, the German breeders have taken this a step further in recent years. They have tried, by means of cross-breeding with Arab thoroughbreds, to make the Haflinger even lighter and therefore more suitable as a riding horse. This cross-breeding of thoroughbreds was condemned by the World Haflinger Union in 1976, and they demanded that these so-called "Arab-Haflingers" should not be included in the Haflinger studbooks.

This tiny filly, standing next to her mother, is only a few weeks old. Curious but distrustful, she stares at this strange person with his camera.

An itchy coat - the horses roll to remove superfluous or tangled hair and to scratch any inaccessible places on their back (above).

This stallion with the wide blaze feels threatened in his territory. He confronts the intruder angrily (opposite).

Unmistakably Haflingers: blonde, flowing manes, small ears and smooth, powerful croup.

The human intruder is observed with a watchful gaze.

Not until he is certain that the newcomer is harmless does the Haflinger stallion resume grazing.

Even when there is thick snow and bitterly cold conditions these young stallions at the Ebbs breeding centre spend a few hours outside every day. As a result of this harsh upbringing, they become very tough and develop an excellent constitution.

In high spirits they gallop through the snow, oblivious to the cold and wet. The uniformity of the colour and markings of the Tirol Haflingers is always attractive, but it is particularly important for the carriage driver, as it makes it easy for him to pick a matching team.

A few games and mock fights with friends also helps to keep warm in this weather.

At the turn of the century this small, strong horse was only widely known, and, indeed, widespread, in the relatively small area of the Tirol. Since 1945 the breeding and distribution of the Haflinger have gained momentum. Haflingers are now found throughout Europe, as well as in the USA, Australia, Africa and Asia. In addition to Austria, there are many studs in Germany, where approximately 6,000 Haflingers are recorded by breeders' associations. There are other Haflinger breeders' associations in Italy, Switzerland, the Netherlands, Belgium, Luxembourg, Denmark, Sweden, France, the United Kingdom and Yugoslavia. Haflingers are also bred in Turkey, Albania, the Czech and Slovak Republics and the former USSR. In these countries they are also used to introduce thoroughbred blood into the indigenous breeds of horses.

The Haflingers also voyaged overseas fairly early on in their relatively short history. The first Haflingers were exported to the USA in 1958, and there are also Haflinger studs in Canada and Brazil.

The Haflingers are regarded as particularly significant in Asia - in recent years a large number of stallions and mares have been exported to India, Bhutan and Thailand to contribute to the refinement of the native packhorse breeds. There, even at heights of 5,000 metres, they display good reactions and stamina compared to the native ponies and mules, and both pure-breeding and cross-breeding will increase in these countries over the next few years.

So, from a tiny corner of the Alps, these blonde horses have conquered the entire world.

The concentrated power of a Haflinger herd.

An impressive stallion: clear eyes and a fine head.

The occasional gallop with the rest of the herd ensures that the horses stay in peak condition.

A mirror image of
a Haflinger:
drinking at a
mountain pool.